DATE DUE

AP 13 '85	JE 24 '86	DE 18 '89	OC 8'9
MAY 1 1985	AG 12 '86	MR 6 '90	OC 31 '9
MY 16 '85	OC 16 '86	MR 28 '90	NO 7 '91
MY 16 '85	AP 15 '87	JE 20 '90	AP 30 '92
JE 20 '85	MY 30 '87	JY 5 '90	JY 16 '92
JE 26 '85	JE 23 '87	AG 3 '90	OC 29 '92
AUG 1 1985	JY 1 9 '88	NO 8 '90	JA 2 3 '93
AG 21 '85	OC 1 0 '88	MR 28 '91	MR 1 8 '93
SE 5 '85	JA 4 '89	AP 8 '91	APR 5 '94
NO 04 '85	JY 20 '89	JE 8 '91	JUN 2 '94
NO 21 '85	AG 2 '89	AG 12 '91	JUN 2 '94
JE 13 '86	SE 2 1 '89	SE 9 '91	JUL 14 '94

E
Ebe   Eberts, Marjorie
Pancakes, crackers, and
pizza: a book. . .

EAU CLAIRE DISTRICT LIBRARY

3/20/85 associated Reib. 7⁵⁹

PANCAKES, CRACKERS, AND PIZZA

A BOOK ABOUT SHAPES

By Marjorie Eberts and
Margaret Gisler

Illustrations by Stephen Hayes

Prepared under the direction of Robert Hillerich, Ph.D.

EAU CLAIRE DISTRICT LIBRARY

 CHILDRENS PRESS ™

CHICAGO

76886

To our mothers

Library of Congress Cataloging in Publication Data

Eberts, Marjorie.
  Pancakes, crackers, and pizza.

  (A Rookie reader)
  Summary: The things that Eddie loves to eat all
come in different shapes. Includes a word list.
    [1. Shape—Fiction. 2. Food—Fiction. 3. Vocabulary]
I. Gisler, Margaret.   II. Hayes, Steven, ill.
III. Hillerich, Robert L., 1927-   .   IV. Title.
V. Series.
PZ7.E194Pan 1984   [E]   84-7699
ISBN 0-516-02063-3

Copyright ©1984 by Regensteiner Publishing Enterprises, Inc.
All rights reserved. Published simultaneously in Canada.
Printed in the United States of America
1 2 3 4 5 6 7 8 9 10 R 93 92 91 90 89 88 87 86 85 84

This is Eddy.

Eddy likes to eat, and eat, and eat.

5

Eddy eats round things.

Eddy eats pancakes,

oranges,

and eggs.

12

Eddy eats square things.

13

EAU CLAIRE DISTRICT LIBRARY

Eddy eats crackers,

CRACKERS

CRACKERS

15

meat,

and cheese.

Eddy eats triangles.

20

Eddy eats pizza,

salad,

and watermelon.

Eddy eats circles,

and squares,

25

and triangles.

Eddy eats all shapes.

28

Eddy eats, and eats, and eats.

Eddy looks

like what he eats.

WORD LIST

all	he	round
and	is	salad
cheese	like	shapes
circles	likes	squares
crackers	looks	things
eat	meat	this
eats	oranges	to
Eddy	pancakes	triangles
eggs	pizza	watermelon
		what

About the Authors

Marjorie Eberts and **Margaret Gisler** have spent the last few years collaborating on books dealing with the language arts. Both have had experience as teachers and have masters degrees in reading from Butler University. This is their first Rookie Reader.

About the Artist

Stephen Hayes is a free-lance, humorous illustrator from Cincinnati, Ohio. He received his degree in Fine Arts from Miami University in Oxford, Ohio. Steve has illustrated humorous greeting cards and several books for children. This book is dedicated to his wife, Susan, and his daughter, Sarah.

EAU CLAIRE DISTRICT LIBRARY